G 526

St. Giles's Cathedral

Frontispiece

EDINBURGH

by Albert Mackie

With eight plates in colour
from paintings by
Leonard Squirrell A.R.W.S., R.E

BLACKIE & SON LIMITED
LONDON AND GLASGOW

Blackie & Son Limited
   16/18 William IV Street,
      Charing Cross, London, W.C.2
   17 Stanhope Street, Glasgow

Blackie & Son (India) Limited
   103/5 Fort Street, Bombay

Blackie & Son (Canada) Limited
   Toronto

Printed in Great Britain by Blackie & Son, Ltd., Glasgow

CONTENTS

PLATES

FESTIVAL CITY

"Of course, the real 'star' of this International Festival is the city of Edinburgh!" It was a music critic from Prague whom I first heard make this enthusiastic remark, but I heard it also from Frenchmen, Americans, Germans, Italians and others who came over to enjoy the varied and colourful fare of the Edinburgh International Festival of Music and Drama. All of them acknowledged, with a fervour that took the native's breath away, that here was the natural "theatre" for such an enterprise.

"What a setting!" That was the general exclamation. It was certainly a memorable experience to be present at the grand march of mayors and burgomasters of Europe down the Royal Mile, from St. Giles' to the courtyard of Holyrood Palace, which was a feature of one of the openings. These men from the Continental capitals were visibly moved by their walk in procession, with all the accompaniment of medieval heraldry, through an ancient thoroughfare lined with modern spectators, with the pavements and windows of the High Street and the Canongate rich in sightseers, both Scottish and cosmopolitan. Edinburgh was once again a Continental capital, as she was in days gone by.

Yet here was something which could not happen in the same way anywhere else in the world—a pageant of moderns, many of them in medieval or in eighteenth-century attire with no trace of self-consciousness, through a historic series of streets with its buildings still telling their ancient story, in an old town perched precariously on a narrow ridge, with a castle at one end and a palace at the other, the shapely mass of Arthur's Seat and Salisbury Crags for romantic background, and the Firth of Forth a silver gleaming streak beyond.

The mayors and burgomasters, as they marched, could not fail to note that in the fossilized history amassed on both sides of them were many evidences of old associations with their own countries, for even in the troubled days of the Wars of Independence, in the thirteenth and fourteenth centuries, this town had traded with the merchant towns of Europe, and every here and there is to be found some architectural link with other cities. They must have been struck by the peculiarity of the old town also, with its lavish old mansions rudely crowded by soaring, smoke-blackened tenements, its picturesque bartizans, corbellings and crowstepped gables standing out bravely side by side with industrial and commercial modernity.

Their royal route took them from the vaulted majesty of the restored Gothic cathedral with the golden storm-cock high up on its valiant crown facing the North Sea wind blowing from the east. They wheeled past the Palladian splendour of the Royal Exchange (the City Chambers) and down the causewayed slope between the steepled mass of the Tron Kirk and the baronial dignity of the *Scotsman* building. Electric tramcars stood back in solemn line to give them clear passage across the modern thoroughfare known as " The Bridges ", and on they went past still more flourishes of modernity, only to plunge (where " John Knox's House " protrudes its " juttied " front across the pavement) into a veritable museum of the ages, with narrow " close " jostling narrow " close " and lofty tenement crowding on lofting tenement, and among them the grandiose forms of Moray House and Huntly House and the old-world outline of the Canongate Tolbooth, not to speak of a noble mansion turned house of refuge for the destitute; and thence into the old Sanctuary of Holyrood and the regal forecourt, with, let it be whispered, breweries and gasworks just around the corner. Edinburgh is a city of such contradictions, and to some visitors that is part of its individuality and charm.

There is a word much used nowadays by the Scottish intelligentsia. It is " antisyzygy ". Professor Gregory Smith applied the phrase " Caledonian antisyzygy " to the common tendency in Scottish literature and art to swing suddenly from the sublime to the shockingly realistic. It may be identified as " the yoking of opposites "—the Devil grinning at the elbow of the saint! Edinburgh seems to epitomize the Caledonian antisyzygy, and nowhere more than in the Royal Mile, its ancient centre and heart, a picturesque series of incongruities.

But it is not of the Old Town alone that our visitors have spoken in rhapsodies. For many of them the memories are rather of the New Town—the spacious beauty of George Street, the architectural symmetry of the North Side of Charlotte Square, the walks along the sunlit but wind-whipped terrace of Princes Street, the broad sweep there of the former Nor' Loch valley, from the modern shop-fronts to the Castle on its famous Rock, and the jagged silhouette of the Old Town sloping down to the east against the southern sky. Or perhaps they carry with them a lasting picture of the vistas to east and west along that great street—the National Monument and Nelson's Tower on Calton Hill; the Scott Monument; the spires of the West End outlined against the evening sun.

Perhaps they remember, and not always with distaste, the climatic peculiarities—" the wind and the rain " which gave a sojourner in our midst the title for his play of student life in this city—the mists and the railway smoke rising around the rocky citadel from the former " Dolorous Valley " below. Or they may have gone farther afield, to the opulent suburbs of Grange, Morningside, or Murrayfield, to the wild slopes of the Pentlands or the deep-wooded gorge of the Dean, to the pleasant and beautifully renovated shores of Cramond or the sequestered glades of Hermitage of Braid. There are so many places to go to in a city stretching six miles across from Firth to Pentlands, and with a sea-front of over eight miles, running from the mouth of the River Almond, at the edge of Lord Rosebery's Dalmeny estate, to Magdalene Bridge near Musselburgh. You have the choice here of streets or gardens, sands or hills, museums and libraries or walks along the country roads, without going out of Edinburgh.

True, many of the country parts of Greater Edinburgh are changing their complexion, from ploughed lands and green fields, and acres of waving ripe corn, to rows of houses, under the pressure of an expanding population, but the city does much also in the way of preserving its green pleasure grounds. Its coastal amenities, despite the decline of Portobello for a while, are becoming steadily enhanced. Barnton has preserved its village air on the western boundary. Turnhouse, though now a modern airport, retains its country air.

Gogarburn is still a health-giving retreat for the unfit. Corstorphine, though greatly built over, still invites with its natural zoo-park surroundings and still flaunts its turreted hill with its winding " Rest and Be Thankful " walk, though pylons also adorn its summit. Sighthill has become a big industrial estate with a vast housing scheme, but Juniper Green is as pretty as ever.

To walk the boundaries, round the back of Torphin Hill, Torduff reservoir, lovely Bonally and Capelaw Hill, and along the crest of the Pentlands—Fala Knowe, Allermuir Hill, Byerside Hill, Caerketton, White Hill and the " T " Wood—is to know the wilds as Stevenson knew and loved them. Where Robert Louis roamed with the Roaring Shepherd, Hillend has become a splendid public park easily reached by tramway.

The southern boundary meanders on by Lothian Burn, embracing Straiton, Burdiehouse and Gilmerton among other old Lothian villages, and almost touching Melville Castle on the banks of the North Esk and the treasure-house of Newbattle Abbey. Bending north again, it brings in Fernieside, Little France and the ruins of Craigmillar Castle. It includes coalfields and cornfields side by side in its domain, and its boundary takes in the modern pithead of New Craighall on its way to join the Firth east of breezy Joppa.

So a choice of country walks or runs may have lured our visitors from the town, or they may have taken advantage of the fact that the city is the natural centre of the tourist industry, with roads and transport giving access to the wealth of sightseeing, north, south, east and west—to the Highlands, the Borders, the rugged sea coast, or the land of Robert Burns.

The city has changed a lot through the ages, and if our town planners have their way it may change a lot more. Town planning is an enthusiasm of our age, as it was of the Edinburgh of 1763 which first threw a North Bridge across the valley to open the way from the Old Town, on the main ridge, to the parallel ridge beyond, on which the New Town was to rise in more orderly design. Big changes are planned for the capital of Scotland, but they are still the subject of much debate. Whatever alterations may eventually come to fruition, the unique character of the place cannot fail to remain. Already in the city Greek, Roman, Renaissance and Scotch Baronial architecture flourish side by side, and Functionalism has found its place; but, be the buildings of the future Greek, Functionalist or what they will, the rugged contours of Edinburgh will have the last Gothic laugh, so long as the rocks and ridges remain, so long as the sun shines from the south and the Scottish summer twilight lingers, so long as the winds bluster round the heights and howl up through the valleys.

Our city's shape is predetermined by the elements, and particularly the elements of long ago. Volcanic plugs of formidable basalt stood up against the eastward-drifting grind of the ice-field, and sheltered their sloping ridged tails from the furrowing glacier, which ploughed horseshoe valleys below their western flanks and sculptured out the deep valleys betwixt ridge and ridge. Dynastic ambitions and foreign invasion gave the citadel on the rock, looking out on the sea and keeping a steady vigil on the main approaches from the hostile south, its foremost national importance.

In warring times, Edinburgh was a " natural " for the capital of Scotland once the country had set its boundary far south of Forth. In thanksgiving for its shelter, a Scottish king placed his abbey snugly at the foot of the ridge, in the valley near Arthur's Seat. Burghers multiplied near the protecting castle walls. Princes and peers built their homes and laid out their gardens on the lower slope of the ridge towards the abbey and around the royal court.

Thus a city grew, taking its tribute from sea and country, establishing its contacts with the merchants of Europe and strengthening itself against the envious invader. Commerce inspired and equipped, though family feuds and battling neighbours frequently interrupted, the building of the burgh.

A swiftly multiplying population turned gardens into overcrowded slums, so that the very word " close ", originally meaning a garden enclosure attached to a wealthy house, came in time to mean a narrow passage between congested dwellings. Wisdom contended with haste and necessity, and the exigencies of war, in the building, both of the Old Town, and of the New to which it eventually overflowed. Often wisdom won; but haste and necessity and the exigencies of war also left their marks.

" Citadel of the slope "—that is what the old Celtic name of Edinburgh, " Dunedin ", is said to mean. It is perhaps the most likely derivation of all, though the city has had many names, and these names have had many interpretations. To suggest a fathering by Edwin, the seventh-century king of Northumbria, it became for a while " Edwinesburg ". In the twelfth century it was known also as " Castellum Puellarum ", " Le Castel des Pucèles ", " Maidens' Castle ", and the legend of beautiful Pictish princesses sheltering on the rock (with its many romantic variations), it would be brutal to discard.

The castle on the rock had established itself as a royal refuge by the end of Malcolm Canmore's reign in the late eleventh century, and Malcolm's saintly Saxon queen, a refugee from the Norman Conquest, is credited with building the tiny chapel which sits daintily on the crest of the rock about three hundred feet up from the railway valley—the capital's oldest building, and its most prominently placed.

King David's Augustinian abbey of Holyrood followed in 1128, and Edinburgh was well established as a royal town and seat of government by the time Alexander III, in 1286, left his council chamber here to ferry over to Fife, where he fell to his death on horseback over the cliff at Kinghorn. Early records referring to Edinburgh's status were probably destroyed in the invasions of the Edwards of England, and the earliest extant charter of the city is from the patriot king, Robert the Bruce, in 1329.

It is interesting to note that this charter confirmed the city's possession of the port of Leith, its link with the Continent. Leith had much to do with Edinburgh's subsequent rise, although it was not until 1920 that the town of Leith itself became incorporated in the city, and the long history of rivalry between these two adjacent burghs is still fresh in living memory.

Full official recognition of Edinburgh as a capital came in Stewart times, in the reign of James II (of Scotland), in the fifteenth century. It was now the centre of brilliant courts, but also of intrigues, open disputes and even battles in the High Street and Canongate. From the wild corners of the kingdom came hot-blooded chiefs with their followers to settle their quarrels on the causeway on the ridge. Yet the city grew in merchandise, producing shrewd merchant adventurers, brilliant scholars and poets, and decent burgesses, as well as its gangs of bloodthirsty villains, whose murderous arts were for any man's hire, and its riotous mob, all too responsive to polemical preachers and spirited blackguards. Its prowess in the arts of peace—in building, in the foundation of centres of learning, and in the development of literature and scientific invention—are the more remarkable for its violently troubled history.

Conspicuously, and tragically, the city is associated with the story of Mary Queen of Scots, last of her fated line to rule over Scotland alone, and mother of the first King of Great Britain. Hither she came, a king's young widow from France, to take over her heritage in the face of religious enmity and court intrigue. Here, as an upholder of the Roman faith, she was obliged to suffer the fierce homilies of that spearhead of the Reformation, John Knox, who had begun his campaign against Popery at court, on his return from Geneva, with a savage pamphlet—" The Monstrous Regiment of Women "—against her mother, Mary de Guise, and who was equally prepared to make young Mary's own reign an uneasy one.

Here she lay in constant peril from the intrigues of nobles, who included her own kith and kin; here she married her dastardly cousin, Henry Darnley; here her husband had her Italian secretary, David Rizzio, murdered before her eyes; here Darnley himself was murdered by being blown up, at Kirk of Field where he lay ill of the smallpox; here the town mob besieged her in the Black Turnpike till she turned on them, as mad as Ophelia; here she was cajoled into marrying the uncouth adventurer Bothwell, whom the town rioters accused along with her of the murder of Darnley.

From here she went into abdication and imprisonment, to escape and do hopeless battle for her rights, and then to seek asylum over the Border with her cousin Elizabeth of England, who feared her as a rival for the English Throne and as a potential ally of Spain. That asylum became nineteen years of imprisonment, terminated only by her death on the block at Fotheringhay Castle in 1587.

It was in Edinburgh Castle, whither Mary had gone for refuge, like many of her royal predecessors, that the first King of Britain was born. His eventual ascension to the Throne in the south drew away much of the court life of the city, but the continuance of a Scottish Parliament for a further century maintained its actual status as a capital, and the preservation of a separate judiciary and kirk kept the nation distinct much longer. James's friendship with the Edinburgh jeweller, George Heriot, was to have an important influence on the city's educational facilities.

Edinburgh's riotous mob made its impact on British history when Charles I, and Archbishop Laud, attempted to introduce the Prayer Book into Scottish Churches, and the books and stools thrown at the preacher who " dared to say mass " began the National Covenant movement, which was to cut deeply into the life of the northern nation, and to leave its imprint on the outlook of the people, for many generations to come.

A brave fighter for Charles I was the Marquis of Montrose, and in this same city he was carried to a felon's death after the son of his King had disowned him to placate the powerful Covenanters.

English and Scottish Puritanism came to blows, and, to put the Covenanters in their place, Cromwell invaded Edinburgh by the coast road. His 11,000 Ironsides smashed the 22,000-strong Scottish Army at Dunbar on September 3, 1650, and thereafter, for a grievous spell, the city and its port of Leith were under occupation by the Protector, who brought in English families as settlers, had his Citadel built at the port, and imposed heavy burdens on the citizens, as well as taking sundry pot shots at the Castle to manifest his might.

Charles II left a more pleasing impress on the city, for it is to him that much of the splendour of Holyroodhouse is due. When the Stewarts once again were in exile, Prince Charles Edward, of the ill-starred royal clan, entered Edinburgh in the course of his skilful advance south. This was on September 17, 1745, after he had eluded Sir John Cope's forces with his tartan-clad Highland host. " Bonnie Prince Charlie " failed to take the Castle, but he strutted his short, triumphal hour on the brilliant stage of Holyrood before sallying out to surprise Cope at Prestonpans at dawn on September 21, when 2500 of his Highlanders with drawn swords scattered the 2300 regulars in a matter of minutes, before he crossed the Border with his army of 6000 Highlanders on further triumphs before the retreat at Derby and the death of his hopes on Culloden Moor near Inverness.

Apart from the headlines of history, the eighteenth century brought brave days for Edinburgh. Scottish literature was given a notable revival by Allan Ramsay, barber, wigmaker and bookseller, who had brought his amazing talents from the uplands of Lanarkshire and who was the first since the stern days of early Presbyterianism to make a practical effort at giving Scotland its place in the theatre. His resuscitation of Scottish letters and song paved the way for the great poet, Robert Burns. A still more immediate influence on the Ayrshire man was Ramsay's Edinburgh-born successor, Robert Fergusson, who was born near the Tron Kirk on September 5, 1750, and who had four brilliant years of poetic output, mostly in the Scottish language, before dying in the city madhouse at the age of 25.

Robert Burns himself was to find his fame in Edinburgh. It was the literary men of the Scottish capital who " discovered " him, and he was to experience a warm and heartening reception from the city's wits and intellectuals and cultured gentry. It was, by Burns's time, a place renowned for its philosophers and theologians, its painters and its architects, its well-to-do patrons of the arts and its busy, alert booksellers.

It was also, just as fortunately, a city dominated by men conscious of the greater capabilities of the place. In 1752 the leading men in business and the professions had come together to promote a scheme to extend the burgh, improve the buildings, and open new roads. " Let us boldly enlarge Edinburgh to the utmost!" they cried.

Hence came the Royal Exchange buildings and piazza, the North Bridge, and the beginnings of the New Town, to be followed by a series of extensions distinguished by buildings of outstanding elegance which delight the eye of the visitor to this day. Thus, in the latter half of the eighteenth century and the beginning of the nineteenth, in a matter of forty years, a medieval town, uncannily perched on a ridge, became a handsome and beautifully laid-out metropolis, " the Athens of the North ".

Nor was it to be a metropolis in wealth of buildings and bridges alone. The show of affluence was solidly based on commercial greatness, and the city continued to grow great in the mercantile arts. It was progressing just as conspicuously in the commerce of ideas. From this Edinburgh, Walter Scott, the advocate, emerged as " the Wizard of the North ", to establish himself as a writer of world renown. From here Adam Smith made his name as a great economist. Here Allan Ramsay, the younger, and Sir Henry Raeburn achieved greatness in the art of portraiture; Simpson and Lister (an English incomer), in anæsthetics and aseptic surgery; the brothers Adam, in planning and architecture. In one of the later streets, to the north of the New Town, was born Robert Louis Stevenson.

It was not by accident that such great men emerged from such a city. Such writers as Scott and Stevenson owed their inspiration to the fact that they were born in a city which had become a meeting place of great intellects, and also to the ancient surroundings which predetermined their skill in historical romance. Simpson and Lister, while undeniably great in themselves, owed much to their good fortune in following in a great Edinburgh tradition in medicine and surgery, and the existence of a progressive medical school with good facilities.

We are tempted to dwell on these historic, romantic and cultural aspects, but the industrial and commercial importance of the city must not be overlooked. Situated among coal and shale, it could not fail to be affected by the Industrial Revolution, and with its port towards the Continent it rose to be the biggest town in Scotland, before the vaster development of the Atlantic trade gave Glasgow its greater industrial importance. In Edinburgh, industrial development, and particularly

(G 526)

L.R.Squirrell

G 526

Edinburgh Castle, from Grassmarket

railway development, cut fiercely across town planning and sent many of the schemes of the artistically minded astray. To some visitors, on the other hand, the railway through the old " Dolorous Valley ", and the windy Waverley Steps up from the main station, are among the wonders of the city; and even the juxtaposition of breweries and palace, regarded with disapproval by modern planners, has its perverse admirers. To enumerate the city's trades would take up a good deal of space, but they range from big-scale engineering and rubber manufacture, to woollen textiles, hosiery, printing, the making of wireless sets, and food processing of all kinds. There are, in fact, few forms of industry not represented. Edinburgh has that desirable possession, industrial variety, the best specific against severe depression, the best safeguard against slumps, and its amenities and cheap facilities continue to attract new industrial enterprise.

As for its much discussed weather, Edinburgh's is not (despite what Robert Louis Stevenson, a townsman not blessed with robust health, once wrote) " one of the vilest climates under heaven ". Nor is its Old Town life so Hogarthian as he depicted it (and as it was, to some extent, in his day). On the whole it is a healthy town, with healthy and decent people inhabiting it.

The city receives a good share of sunshine, in winter and in summer. The high terrace of Princes Street, facing the south, basks frequently in the kindly rays; and it is a fine place for a gay stroll. The keen winds are well known, but in hot weather the sea breezes come as a blessing. November and January fogs and " haar ", from the sea and rivers, are notorious; but they are not so frequent as they used to be. The swiftly changing sky is apt to bring rain when it is least expected, and so a light raincoat or an umbrella is a handy thing to carry around even on the best of days. Snow seldom lies long in the salty-aired town, but on the neighbouring hills ski-ing has sometimes been possible, and ponds in the city occasionally yield sport for the skater. " Bracing and invigorating " would best describe the general atmosphere. For those who can brave the boisterous winds and who have a taste for climbing of the less venturesome sort, the views from the heights are incomparable. Now and again there are hot summers when it is a welcome relief to recline on the grassy slopes of West Princes Street

Gardens, or bathe at Cramond or Portobello, where the Pool is the main attraction.

Our citizens are sometimes described as aloof and " cagey ". Many visitors from abroad find them quite the reverse—polite and refined, reserved but friendly, keen on privacy, for themselves and others, but ready with a warm welcome for those who show they desire it. The legendary Edinburgh snob is as much a thing of the past as the riotous mobs who lynched Captain Porteous or flung the kirk stools at the Bishop's head. Here is a well-behaved citizenry, proud of its city and appreciative of those who like it, and happy at all times to participate in the many fine spectacles to which its " own romantic town " lends itself.

THE CASTLE

One of the most popular side-shows on festive occasions is the provision of military displays on the Castle Esplanade, with piping, dancing and exercises in the glare of searchlights placed at strategic points on the ramparts. The frequent illumination of the Castle by great beam-projecting lamps around the rocks and within the walls has been a happy feature since the years between the wars, and the revival of the picturesque practice was one of the most striking signs of the close of hostilities, the end of black-outs and the return to hopeful days of peace after the Second World War.

I remember that when the idea was proposed in the inter-war years there were citizens who protested that the lighting of these well-proportioned buildings from below was "against nature" and æsthetically wrong. The Castle, they said, should be seen in the pale moonlight with the shadows cast downwards; and to throw the shadows upwards was to distort and disfigure the scene. If the objectors remain, they are well in the minority, and strangely silent to-day, for the spectacle of what appears to be a fairy citadel floating in mid-air is admired and welcomed by visitors and citizens alike.

Your visit to the Castle begins at the Esplanade. This was at one time the drilling ground of the garrison, but since the fine commodious barracks at Redford, west of the city, drew full garrisons away from the ancient stronghold, military displays are not so common and are the more exciting when they return. There were times, in the wicked old days, when the Esplanade was a place of execution, and here several covens of witches, who confessed dealings with the Devil in person, were put to the fire.

On the right-hand side of the Esplanade, as you walk towards the Castle, there is an admirable equestrian statue of Earl Haig, the World War I general who was born in the city. Beyond the railings on this side the green hill slopes down to the Princes Street valley, where once lay the western stretch of the Nor' Loch, latterly a noisome marsh which refined citizens were glad to see completely filled in and ornamented over a hundred years ago, to give us the pleasant and elegant Princes Street Gardens.

As you cross the Castle moat (dry and paved) by the drawbridge, which may be guarded by a kilted sentry, you find in great niches on the two sides of the outer portal the large-scale statues of the two men who led resistance against the mighty Edwards of England in the thirteenth- and fourteenth-century Wars of Independence—Sir William Wallace and King Robert the Bruce. These stalwart and challenging figures, decorating the front wall of a fortress which bulked prominently in these conflicts, are modern additions to the ornamentation. King George VI and Queen Elizabeth, as Duke and Duchess of York, attended the unveiling of these statues on 28th May, 1929, to celebrate the 600th anniversary of the granting of a charter to Edinburgh by King Robert the Bruce. A Captain Hugh Reid in 1832 left a thousand pounds to be placed at interest to accumulate as a fund to assist in erecting some memorial to these national heroes in such a place, and so it was very nearly a hundred years before the original donor's dream was realized. In the making of the statues, Scotland and England shared the honours, since the Wallace is by Alexander Garrick of Edinburgh and the Bruce by Thomas J. Clapperton of London.

It was to take the Castle from the English for Robert the Bruce that Randolph, Earl of Moray, led a party of climbers up the Rock from the northern valley in 1312. Formidable as the Rock seems, it has not been unknown for soldiers in the garrison to find a way down to see their sweethearts, and a way back up again to slip in unobserved, and it was a Scottish soldier of such enterprise who showed Bruce's army the way. On the other side, a rock formation known as the Kittle Nine Steps used to be a favourite " henner " (dare) of High School boys, and Sir Walter Scott himself, as a cripple youngster, shared in the distinction of performing it.

The last time I saw the Rock climbed was by a party of student mountaineers who were doing it for charity, but it is a feat that is naturally not encouraged by the police.

Inside the Castle walls the sights which have been pointed out and

G 526

Entrance, Scottish National War Memorial

explained to visitors for generations are St. Margaret's Chapel, our earliest record of Edinburgh's beginnings; the great cannon, "Mons Meg"; the restored Argyll Tower with its dungeons above the portcullis gate, once a state prison similar to those in the Tower of London; the old Parliament Hall; and the part erected in 1555 where Mary Queen of Scots went for refuge, from the enemies and spies who plagued her at Holyrood, and where James VI of Scotland and I of England was born. On the Castle's topmost parapet is the iron fire-basket which was used for beacons, signalling news from point to point in the days before newspapers, telegraph and the radio. Now the chief attraction of the old Palace Yard or Crown Square is the Scottish National War Memorial, surely one of the most perfect expressions anywhere of a nation's respect for its heroic dead.

In the centre of the Palace block is the stone-vaulted Crown Chamber or Jewel Room, which displays the Honours of Scotland—the Scottish Regalia and other jewels. These treasures have had a varied history and many travels. A Scottish Crown was carried off to England by Edward I after his defeat of John Balliol, but Bruce made a Crown for himself. The Scottish Crown we now have consists largely of the material of the Bruce Crown made after 1314—the year of the Battle of Bannockburn, in which King Robert established himself and his nation. James V of Scotland ordered its completion in 1540, and with this Crown the hapless Mary was made Queen when she was nine months old. Its craftsmanship is a mixture of French and Scottish, with carbuncles, jacynths, amethysts, topazes, crystals and pearls set in gold and enamel around the velvet cap. Scottish pearls and Scottish gold (from Crawford Moor in Lanarkshire) are included in the materials.

To keep these jewels out of the hands of Cromwell after his victory at Dunbar, they were smuggled off to Dunnottar Castle, and they lay buried for a time beneath the floor of the parish church of Kinneff until the Restoration of Charles II. After the Union of Parliaments in 1707 they were sealed up in a chest in the Crown Chamber.

A Royal Commission of 1794 authorized selected persons to break into the Chamber and investigate if the Crown and its pertinents were there. The authorized gentlemen broke open the door, but retired without opening the chest, as a punctilious member said they were not authorized to do this. It was twenty-four years before the experiment was repeated, but this time, on the 4th February, 1818, the Commissioners broke open the chest, and, in the words of Lord Cockburn, "found the Regalia sleeping beneath the dust that had been gathering upon them ever since the Union". Sir Walter Scott was a leader in this rediscovery of the Honours, yet when John Kemble the actor said to the Wizard, "Is not that a splendid Crown?" Scott is reported to have replied, "The last time I saw you as Macbeth, you had a much grander one!"

It was Scott's patriotic passion for Scottish antiquities that secured the return to the Castle, in 1829, of Mons Meg, the grand old battered cannon which points out over the ramparts towards the city and the firth, and which nurses at its side some old cannon-balls which may or may not have been fired from it. The cannon is 13 feet long with a 2 ft. 3½ in. bore, and is reputed to have been made by Scottish craftsmen for James II for use at the siege of Thrieve Castle in Galloway in 1455. It was further employed in the siege of Dumbarton in 1488 and in the civil war in 1571. Two men are said to have died in helping to pull it from the Tron Kirk to the Castle. Its name has been variously interpreted—Mount's Meg is one version, but Scott believed it was Mollance Meg, associated with Mollance in Galloway, and named perhaps after its chief artificer's wife. It is an old friend of Edinburgh children, who love to clamber on to it or to hear their voices echo in its deep throat. Until Scott agitated for its return, it had lain in the Tower of London since 1758—a hostage for the city's better behaviour after the Porteous lynching.

And now to that awe-inspiring Memorial—the chief magnet of visitors to the Castle in our time. We of Edinburgh, ourselves, never tire of visiting it, for it would take more than a lifetime to appreciate to the full its many beauties of thought and expression. It takes its place among those rare works of art, such as great novels and plays, great canvases and musical masterpieces, in which every reading, view or hearing uncovers some new wonder. To Scots, naturally, including Scots from overseas, it has a strong personal appeal in its records of the regiments in which they served, or of their friends and kin among the fallen; but as Scotland's tribute in stone to her sons and daughters who died not simply in the cause of Empire, but also for the sake of peace and the betterment of life for all mankind, it has far more than a local, much more than a national, importance.

This was the great task for which Sir Robert Lorimer was chosen, and for which he in his turn gathered together his great band of inspired helpers. There he was given the quadrangle of the medieval palace which had housed royalty until James IV erected Holyroodhouse for his English bride in 1503, and out of the Billings' Barrack building facing the Banqueting Hall he was to shape something new and great. The stones of the older building (in its turn a medieval chapel, an armoury and magazine, and a barracks of the eighteenth century with later alterations) are incorporated in the Memorial, so that there are parts of this sacred edifice which were dedicated to St. Mary as long ago as the reign of David I. Part of the tremendous effect of the Memorial—though to attempt to analyse its beauty is a hopeless venture—radiates from the virile stonework, in keeping with the general ruggedness of the Castle scene. Lorimer had to make his monument with due regard to local misgivings about the " sky-line ", and it says much for his artistry that he was able to alter his original designs to pay attention to such requirements and yet produce something which could not be bettered. He died in 1929, two years after the completion of this, his greatest work, and it is as much a monument to a great architect, and a giant among directors of craftsmen, as it is to his countrymen and countrywomen whom he so magnificently commemorated.

This is shrine-building as it was carried out in the best phases of the Middle Ages, for a whole army of genius went into its erection. Two hundred artists, craftsmen and labourers performed this immense symphony in stone under Lorimer's baton and to his score. They wrought perfectly in stone, wood, metal and glass. " A Coronach in Stone ", it has been called, but if it is a Coronach it is such as could be played only by a MacCrimmon of MacCrimmons. The true Coronach, certainly, is no mere mournful blowing of the pipes, but a masterly composition with groundwork, variations and a crowning last movement, and these are all explicit in these stones. Yet all comparisons, parallels and figures of speech drawn from other arts seem inadequate.

The rugged walls have become one with the solid rock and green turf from which they soar to the sky. The great statuary on the outer walls representing the Motions of the Spirit of Man are as spiritual as anything that ever was chiselled out of stone. The Hall of Honour achieves the impossible by paying a fitting tribute to the great Scottish Divisions whose four badges, with the badges of the component corps, adorn its walls. Symbols of Scotland, the lion and the unicorn, St. Andrew the patron saint, and the lion again triumphant on the top of the crowstepped gable, blend harmoniously with universal themes— the Survival of the Spirit rising from the ashes of the Phoenix, that breath-taking composition in the deep niche above the Great Porch; and, in the Shrine, the great carved figure of the Archangel Michael suspended above the Roll of the Illustrious Dead in its ark pinnacled upon an outcrop of rock. The light in the Shrine from the stained-glass windows accentuates the holiness of the ground we tread on. Could King David I himself, that Sair Sanct (expensive saint) for the Scottish Crown, behold this marvel of modern dedication, he would gaze in awe and wonderment, and find it difficult to believe that such a memorial came from funds offered willingly from the pockets of Scots, rich and poor, and not mulcted in taxation. The Memorial in fact cost £150,000, and every penny of that was raised by subscription. Its erection between the years 1924 and 1927 (it was dedicated in the presence of Edward, Prince of Wales, on the 14th July of the latter year) gave Edinburgh, already acknowledged to be a beautiful and artistic city, its greatest beauty and its greatest cultural possession.

Two other modern developments of the use of the Castle fall to be noted. One is the revival of the Banqueting Hall, or part of it, as a place for State banquets. It was the Rt. Hon. Arthur Woodburn, in his term of office as Secretary of State for Scotland, who conceived the commendable idea of having some place of historic interest and ancient dignity in which to entertain distinguished guests of the nation. The former Governor's House of the now defunct Calton Jail, adjacent to St. Andrew's House, the home of Scottish administration in Waterloo Place, was one place considered for this purpose, but Mr. Woodburn eventually decided on the Lower Banqueting Hall, where, among the time-honoured stones and burnished arms of former ages, with an old-world fire diffusing its warmth from the open hearth, many distinguished visitors have since enjoyed State hospitality. I once had the pleasure of sharing the experience with a band of American newspaper editors, and their reactions were indescribably enthusiastic. Naturally it did not detract from their enjoyment of this unusual meal to learn that their place of entertainment was the scene of the infamous Black Dinner of 1440 at which the placing of a black bull's head upon the table was the signal for the Earl of Douglas and his younger brother, guests of the ten-year-old King, James II, to be dragged from the feast and foully murdered. These pleasantries are not part of the State hospitality to-day.

The other praiseworthy innovation is the tasteful and educative Services museum which is gradually being built up in the edifice along the west side of the Palace Yard.

One of Edinburgh's cherished possessions is the One O'clock Gun. It is fired from the Half-moon Battery at the Castle, built in the formation its name indicates, on the summit of the old St. David's Tower. There has been a battery there for over three hundred years, but its function to-day is not defensive or intimidating, but the firing of the daily time check, by which citizens set their watches, and also the firing of salutes.

A Major of the Red Army who visited Edinburgh in the course of the Second World War indicated to me that he thought very little of the Castle as a fortification. Strangely enough, the same opinion was expressed by a group of high Soviet officers who were shown round it on another occasion. But the Germans thought it worthy of bombs in their Zeppelin raid on the city in 1916, and one of their missiles did hit the Rock, while there was damage and loss of life in the Grassmarket just to the south.

But the comments of modern Russian military men on the Castle have their entertaining aspect. Sir Philip Christison, who was G.O.C.-in-C. Scottish Command and Governor of the Castle at the time of one Soviet visit, enjoys the memory of the old soldier who was asked at the Drawbridge by one of the U.S.S.R. " brass-hats " if he had ever been in Russia. The old Scot replied, with no intention to offend, " Ay, I was owre there chasing thae Bolsheviks!"

Which reminds me that I have omitted to mention one constant joy of the Castle visitor—the Castle guides! These veterans of many wars and campaigns have the old soldier's flair for entrancing story-telling. Turn an attentive face to them and you will hear the history of the place in its most palatable form. If there is a certain amount of ornamentation encrusting the original story, just you try telling the same facts time after time without variation! To my taste, these men are worth every penny they get.

THE ROYAL MILE

Here and there down the Royal Mile you will find by the kerb the high stone wells from which the water caddies used to carry, on their leather-clad backs, with straps over their shoulders, the buckets of water which were, until late in the eighteenth century, the only supply of this indispensable commodity to the homes of rich and poor in the Old Town. They scurried across the streets and up the narrow stairs with their precious supplies every day except Sunday, when the gentlefolk had to make do with stale water.

On Castle Hill, at the start of your journey down the Royal Mile from the Castle to Holyrood, is the reservoir which fed these wells in the days before water was " laid on " in the tenements. To this reservoir the water came five miles across country in a three-inch pipe from the quaint reservoir which still survives on the lands of Comiston beyond the Braid Burn, south of the city towards the Pentland Hills, almost below Robert Louis Stevenson's beloved summer residence at Swanston.

At the corner of the road which winds down from Castle Hill towards the Mound and the New Town stands the Outlook Tower, well worth a visit for the " camera obscura " which presents a series of admirable views of the surrounding sights—the Castle, Ramsay Gardens, Princes Street, Inchkeith out in the Firth of Forth, Fife, the High Street, the South Side and the Pentlands. It is the ideal place for a " quick look " at Edinburgh, and the views projected on the table from the periscope tower enable the competent lecturer on the spot to point out to you some of the principal features of the city. The museum on other floors is likewise instructive concerning the growth of the town. It was a favourite foster-child of the late Sir Patrick Geddes, philosopher of the development of cities, whose talks in these very rooms used to elucidate with astounding skill the mysteries of Edinburgh's own evolution.

27

One of the nearby eminences which make an impressive show in the camera is the 240-foot spire of Tolbooth St. John's Church, which, along with the Free Church close at hand on the corner of Johnston Terrace, is a hive of activity when the assemblies of the various Presbyterian kirks are in session. The principal General Assembly is that of the Church of Scotland, the national church, which, visited by the King's Lord High Commissioner (often a prince or a peer, but in recent times a Labour M.P., who might be a former miner or railwayman), holds its "sederunts" mainly in the great Assembly Hall facing the Mound but with doors letting out on the Royal Mile near the Outlook Tower.

Castle Hill leads into Lawnmarket, a short broad street with many closes and courts off it rich in historic associations, and with one attractive feature in the preservation of, and modern use made of, some of the old high tenements or "lands". Conspicuously, Gladstone's Land, preserved by the National Trust, is the appropriate home of the Saltire Society, a cultural organization which acts as a centre of inspiration and encouragement for much of the native literary and artistic activity of our day. To attend a lecture or a "ceilidh" in this grand old building, with its open beam ceilings painted with fruits, fronds and other flourishes, is to taste something of the life of the brilliant if overcrowded Edinburgh of the eighteenth century and earlier. The "land", which somewhere inside displays the date 1620, was the one-time home of Sir Robert Bannatyne, but it is from Thomas Gladstone, merchant burgess, who acquired it in 1631 and had his initials placed prominently on the gable, that it derives its present name. Its outside stair and its arcades are rare features.

Hard by, in Baxter's Close, Burns shared the room and bed of his friend Richmond, a lawyer's clerk, on the occasion of the poet's triumphal visit to the burgh in 1786, in the house of Mrs. Carfrae, with his window looking into Lady Stair's Close. And there, also, are history and romance. Elizabeth, when Dowager Countess of Stair, was a leader of fashion in her day. Her picturesque old house has the inscription over the porch, "Feare the Lord and depart from evill", the date 1622, and the initials of Sir William Gray, a man of great influence in the days of Charles I, and his lady Egidia, daughter of a provost of the town in 1643.

East Princes Street from Castle Ramparts
Argyll Tower in Foreground

Across the street from this part of the Lawnmarket you will find
Brodie's Close, which takes its name from the plausible scoundrel
who became the hero of a play by Henley and Stevenson and was
possibly the prototype of Stevenson's " Jekyll and Hyde ", Deacon
William Brodie. No doubt he was a low rascal, but there is some
appeal about the man who gets away with a masquerade, and Deacon
Brodie was Raffles and all the other gentlemen thieves of fiction and
romance rolled into one. Successfully he imposed upon his fellow-
citizens, in his trade of cabinet-maker and in his capacities as deacon
of the wrights and masons and a member of the Town Council, as the
apex of respectability, until his daring robbery at the Excise Office
in 1788 brought to light his long career of housebreaking and thieving
under arms. How he managed it in such a small town, as Edinburgh
then was, will ever be a mystery to me. How he contrived to play his
loaded dice in the gambling club he frequented in the Fleshmarket
Close, without " the whole town talking ", I shall never know, for
even with its much multiplied population of to-day, Edinburgh is not
the kind of place where it is easy for a prominent public man to keep
his delinquent tendencies a secret. But the fact is that this gangster
contrived to keep his end up under the daily scrutiny of respectability
while he went around taking moulds and making copies of keys for
the purpose of wholesale robbery. The Exchequer Office in Chessel's
Court he visited quite openly with a friend, studied the lay-out of the
cashier's room, took a putty impression of the outer-door key which
hung on a nail, and later tried his home-made key in the lock. Thereafter he reverted to model citizenship, until on March 5, with his gang,
armed with pistols, he raided the office to steal, not the haul of thousands he expected, but sixteen pounds! How he was surprised in the
act, but evaded the late-comer; how he attempted to establish his
alibi by spending the night with a paramour; how—after an English
outlaw among his associates, wishing to mend his fortunes with the
police, had " tipped them off " and taken them to see Brodie's cache
of keys for future jobs at the foot of the Crags—they chased him all
the way to Amsterdam and brought him home that August, to face
his trial at the High Court and dangle on the hangman's rope in the
High Street in October, reads like a modern thriller except for that

public hanging. Legend, which likes to add its thrills to the sordid lives of such scoundrels, avers that he was the first victim of a new gallows of his own invention.

As we leave the Lawnmarket and enter the High Street, on our right are the County Buildings, and on our left is the handsome Sheriff Court. I once heard a retiring American Consul General tell his successor, " Over here you've got to learn that a Sheriff is not a policeman; he's a judge!" In an office in this building the Procurator Fiscal, whom the Americans would call the District Attorney, prepares his indictments to bring accused persons before the Sheriff; and wigged and gowned advocates ply between this building and the Higher Courts in Parliament Square across the way.

St. Giles' and Parliament Square bring us to the real heart of the city—and, from the legal point of view, the heart of the country. Here, on the causeway in front of the Buccleuch statue, are paving stones arranged in the shape of a heart, and that, for modern Edinburghers, is the Heart of Midlothian. But in Sir Walter Scott's time the Heart of Midlothian was the by-name of the old jail which stood there, and whose ground plan is commemorated in outline by a series of metal blocks in the roadway, with various dates engraved on them. These give an idea of how the old Bellhouse or Tolbooth—the " Heart of Midlothian " which gave a title to Scott's novel about Jeanie Deans and the Porteous Riots, and which was torn down in 1817 after serving as royal court, parliament, council house and eventually prison—used to conceal the handsome porch of the High Kirk, and jutted out into the street to make it somewhat narrower than it is to-day. It was from here that Captain Porteous, commander of the City Guard, was dragged from his cell to play the unenviable role in the most remarkable lynching in the town's often violent and lawless history. This was the sequel to his ordering the guard to open fire on an unruly crowd at a public hanging. Fatalities led to his being tried and sentenced to death, but it was the rumour that he was likely to be reprieved which led the mob to take the law into its own hands and string him up before the friends he was presumed to have " in high places " could do anything about it. The skill with which Scott wove this, and the smuggling incidents which led up to it, into a great novel of Edinburgh life is nowadays rather taken for granted, but for a picture of the city as it had been not very long before his own time, *The Heart of Midlothian* would be hard to surpass.

" Tolbooth ", a word which occurs at various places in the city, originally meant a place for the payment of taxes. In the fourteenth century the tolbooth stood where the Thistle Chapel now is, at the other end of St. Giles', in the common vennel leading to the church-yard and burial ground, of which the only trace now is the stone lettered " I.K. " in metal, marking the grave of " Iohannes " Knox, the kirk's most famous minister. That old tolbooth was wiped out in an English invasion in 1385, and the Bellhouse, the new tolbooth, was erected in 1386 at the site which the Heart now indicates. How it housed the royal court and the Scottish Parliament is difficult to comprehend, as its outline does not suggest space to swing a cat in.

Majestic, Gothic St. Giles', with its confident crown steeple of eight flying buttresses, has also been many things in its day. There was a time when the General Assembly of the Church of Scotland held its " sederunts " there, but it served secular purposes as well, for when the Tolbooth was condemned in 1560 as a town house, both the Town Clerk's office and the Court of Session moved into the kirk, and the Town Clerk's office was still there early in the nineteenth century. The history of the kirk goes back to the ninth century at least, but it received its Norman shape in 1126, frequent invasions interrupting the work and forcing it to continue in stages over a long period. It was a collegiate church in Roman Catholic days, and it became the headquarters of the Reformers, who cleared it of " Popish " interior decorations in the early frenzies of Puritanical fanaticism. John Knox thundered from its pulpit as its first Protestant minister.

Here it was that Archbishop William Laud's Scottish edition of the Prayer Book was read out to the congregation in July 1638 with disastrous results. According to the contemporary account, " some religious men and women of all sorts did so hate it that they would not permit it to be read in Edinburgh, and first at the reading of the said service book the good religious women did rise up to the reader and flung their books and their stools at him and did rive all the service books apieces, and the Bishop of Edinburgh, called Mr. David Lindsay, was so stoned with the wives and knocked that he was forced to fly to a stair benorth the Cross and did wend up, otherwise they had killed him. So this did begin the Troubles of Scotland."

That was the start of the Covenanting movement, but nowadays St. Giles' is a graceful and calm ecclesiastical centre, distinguished for excellent church music and choral singing, and with an opulence of interior decoration which would have horrified its early Calvinistic spring-cleaners. Fortunately the City Fathers have long recognized its dignity and central importance, and have gone out of their way to preserve and repair it and make it a place worthy of a capital city. Between 1829 and 1833 its exterior was repaired and improved at a cost of £21,600. That great enthusiast for city improvements, Lord Provost Chambers, sponsored, and supported from his private means, a substantial restoration in 1870. The Thistle Chapel, yet another example of the brilliant teamwork of artists and craftsmen under the inspired leadership of Sir Robert Lorimer, restored to St. Giles' in our own day something of the enthusiastic church-building of pre-Reformation times.

In front of St. Giles' down the line of the High Street used to run the Luckenbooths, a series of shop buildings, and between them and the kirk were the Krames—an arcade of stalls where Henry Cockburn in boyhood spent his New Year farthings among a rich array of fascinating toys in a glittering Aladdin's cave—"like one of the Arabian Nights' bazaars in Baghdad".

Further congesting the main thoroughfare in those days were the Mercat Cross, whose successor, the gift of Mr. Gladstone, now stands aside in Parliament Square, and the old City Guard House, barracks of the picturesque Highland veterans who kept the peace of the streets, armed with muskets and Lochaber axes, and who were abolished in November 1817 with the establishment of a real force of police. Police headquarters are now in High Street and Parliament Square, very near to where the old City Guard had their offices.

Parliament Square is rich in history, but is probably just as interesting to-day as it ever was; for it is the home of the law, the centre of that distinct justiciary which helps to preserve something of Scotland's separate nationhood, and the training ground and meeting point

G 526

White Horse Close, Cannongate

of the bewigged advocates engaged in criminal and civil cases. Many distinguished men have walked its grand hall. Not the least famous of its advocates was Sir Walter Scott. Least successful of its advocates, as an advocate, was that other great literary figure bred by this city, Robert Louis Stevenson, who was no more cut out for the legal career he chose for himself, than for the engineering career which his sorely tried father had hoped he would follow.

As its name indicates, Parliament House, built in 1633–40 at a cost of £10,000, housed the Scottish Parliament until that body was incorporated in the English Parliament in the Treaty of Union, 1707. It was also used regularly as a town hall until the early years of last century, and its history as a court house had already begun before the Union. Close at hand is the former Advocates' Library, now the National Library of Scotland, a rich repository of print and manuscripts, with, in the same vicinity, the valuable Signet Library associated with the Writers to the Signet. They are appropriately near to the old literary centre of Scotland, for in the neighbourhood of St. Giles' were bookshops closely connected with the intellectual life of the town in its brightest eras.

Parliament Close, as it then was, was the haunt of jewellers, watchmakers, and librarians, and the most famous Edinburgh jeweller of all, George Heriot, otherwise known as Jingling Geordie, friend of Britain's first King and Queen, and founder of George Heriot's School, had his little shop and forge in this quarter. Another of the city's great educational benefactors, James Gillespie, of a much later period, is commemorated farther down the High Street, across the way, by a caricature-like plaque of his large-nosed profile at the site of his snuff and tobacco shop. He it was of whose fabulous property the rhyme went—

> " Wha wad hae thocht it,
> That noses bocht it ?"

Facing Parliament Square, on the other side of the High Street, are the municipal buildings. Advocates' Close, where the Lighting and Cleansing Department has its club rooms, has associations with Dr. Johnson and his biographer Boswell of Auchinleck, and from

3

this opening to Anchor Close stretch the city departments—City Engineer's office, Lighting and Cleansing Department, a mass radiography unit behind in Writers' Court, the Dean of Guild Court, the Electoral Registration Officer and Surveyor of Water Rates, the City Assessor's Office and the premises of the City Collector and Local Taxation Officer. Beyond the arches and the city War Memorial, and the open square where Alexander tries to calm Bucephalus in a muscular sculptured group, is the entrance to the City Chambers, where the Town Council deliberates at regular sessions and where also it lavishly entertains its distinguished guests, and there the Lord Provost and the Town Clerk have their offices.

The buildings, originally designed as the Royal Exchange to give the merchants a better meeting place than at the Mercat Cross in the open air, form one of our builders' many triumphs over the problems presented by the steep slopes on which the city is founded. While the front elevation in the High Street presents the appearance of a building of moderate height, the rear elevation facing Cockburn Street near the Waverley Bridge has the aspect of a " skyscraper ". The foundation stone of the Royal Exchange was laid in September 1753, and the place was to accommodate some forty shops, three coffee-houses, ten dwellings, a customs house and a piazza. Adam Smith, the famous economist, had his office in the Custom House on the second floor, but the Custom House was vacated in 1809. On May 14, 1811, the Town Council crossed the street from its inadequate residence in the precincts of St. Giles' and took possession of the Exchange for its City Chambers. Late in the nineteenth century, after an open competition for a design, adjacent properties were acquired, shops were demolished, and handsome arches formed; and the foundations of the new portions were laid in 1901, the new City Chambers being opened in January 1904.

The south side of the High Street between Parliament Square and the Tron Church was the scene of disastrous fires in June and November 1824, which destroyed a series of high buildings stretching from the High Street to the Cowgate, and involved the steeple of the Tron Kirk itself. After the November fire a tenement wall 130 feet high had to be pulled down by a party of English sailors brought from a frigate in Leith Roads; they took two days to get it down, and another high wall had to be blown up. It was in the course of the hour-long brilliant blaze in which the Tron Kirk's old Dutch steeple of wood, iron and ornamented lead went up in flames, that Sir Walter Scott, in the broad Scots which he frequently spoke, exclaimed—" Eh, sirs, mony a weary, weary sermon hae I heard beneath that steeple!" To replace the Dutch steeple, an elegant stone spire was erected in 1828. There were those who said that these disastrous fires were divine punishment on the city for its having dared to accommodate a musical festival!

" Christ's Church at the Tron ", to give it its full title, was built in 1637. The Tron from which it took its name was a public beam for the weighing of merchandise—also used as a pillory and a place of punishment and execution! Here ears were nailed and tongues were bored for the crimes of falsehood and cheating. Now the Tron Kirk, to Edinburgh folk, is the principal rendezvous for open-air celebrations at Hogmanay (New Year's Eve), and it is around this corner that the milling crowds forgather to hail with cheers and song and the drinking of toasts the movement of the minute hand of the great clock to the hour of midnight and the beginning of a new year. From this point they disperse to start on their rounds of " first-footing ".

A side street to note near the Tron, cutting through from the High Street, across Cockburn Street and down several flights of steps to the Waverley Station, is Fleshmarket Close, whose name is reminiscent of the eighteenth-century days when the fleshers did their slaughtering on the north bank of the Nor' Loch where the Waverley Station now has a suburban platform.

In the portion of the High Street beyond " The Bridges " there is a quaintly named World's End Close. Near it is Tweeddale Court, scene of a murder mystery which was one of the sensations of the early part of last century. The British Linen Company had its premises there, and on the 13th November, 1806, its messenger was stabbed to death in the lane leading from the court, the murderer getting away with over £4000 in notes of large denomination. The booty was later unearthed in the grounds of Bellevue to the north-east of the New Town, but the murderer was never discovered, although various theories as to his identity were published.

" John Knox's House ", on the left as we walk towards the Canongate, is a striking survival of the street architecture of the reformer's period, but the commonly held supposition that it housed the man himself is not well authenticated. Near it was the Netherbow, the principal gate of the city, where, until 1856, the city's jurisdiction was limited by the wall which marked it off from the adjacent burgh of the Canongate.

The Canongate (the Canons' road from the Abbey) was the court quarter and residence of the nobility. Its Tolbooth, an ornate building dating from 1591, stands out in picturesque silhouette low down the hill on this north side, and in the churchyard nearby are the graves of famous men, among them the philosopher Dugald Stewart and the poet Robert Fergusson, whose stone was raised in generous tribute by his successor in vernacular rhyming, Robert Burns.

Breweries, gasworks and railway lines have invaded the former gardens of some of the nobility, but several of the old mansions remain to indicate what the burgh must have looked like, and preservation and restoration of such properties, and their adaptation for cultural purposes, have been commendable features of civic policy.

Moray House, with its graceful balcony, fronts the Edinburgh Provincial Training College for Teachers and its demonstration school. Huntly House is a city museum. Queensberry House became a house of refuge for the destitute after being, in Cockburn's words, " the brilliant abode of rank and fashion and political intrigue ". The last gentleman to occupy it as a mansion, Sir James Montgomery, Lord Chief Baron and author of the Entail Act, died in 1803.

In Dunbar's Close on the left, Cromwell and his Ironsides had their guardhouse. Panmure Close sheltered the seventeenth-century mansion in which at one time Adam Smith resided. The gardens of Reid's Court and Campbell's Close suggest how the by-ways of the Canongate may have looked before overcrowding developed. Whitefoord House is a kind of Scottish version of Chelsea Hospital—the Scottish Naval and Military Veterans' Residence—and Whitehorse Close preserves a fine example of an old Edinburgh courtyard.

Beyond the Watergate (" road to the sea ") we enter the old Sanctuary of Holyrood, which really was a sanctuary for debtors and other fugitives until 1880, and now we step into the precincts of the Palace.

Holyrood Palace from base of Salisbury Crags

L. R. Squirrell

G 526

Horse Wynd nearby was one of the few side streets in the old days wide enough to permit a horse to pass through, and for a time it was nicknamed " Cavalry Lane ".   In the eighteenth century the genteel families had their beautiful houses there.

Holyrood Road, running parallel to Canongate on its southern side, was formerly the South Back Canongate.   Farther west the Cowgate runs parallel to the High Street and many of the High Street closes slope down into it.   In the names of the Canongate and the Cowgate the word " gate " means a road (the word for an actual gate in Edinburgh place-names is " port "), and the Cowgate originated as a lane round the back of the burgh used by the herdsmen driving their cattle to and from the Burgh Muir, the grazings south of the city walls. The valley of the Cowgate is traversed by modern thoroughfares over George IV Bridge and South Bridge.   At the end of the eighteenth century the gully underwent a swift transition from centre of fashion to " the last retreat of destitution and disease ", but slum clearances between the two World Wars much improved it, though as the lodging-house quarter it continued to be the refuge of the down-and-out.   Two hundred years ago, by contrast, its St. Cecilia's Hall, a beautiful concert room, was " the most selectly fashionable place of amusement ", where Henry Cockburn saw " most of our literary and fashionable gentlemen, predominating with their side curls, and frills, and ruffles, and silver buckles;   and our stately matrons stiffened in hoops and gorgeous satin, and our beauties with high-heeled shoes, powdered and pomatum'd hair, and lofty and composite head-dresses ".

Cardinal Beaton had his turreted mansion at the corner of Blackfriars Wynd, where Blackfriars Street now ends, and in this same quarter the Princess Elizabeth St. Clair of Roslin came to her town house preceded by eighty lighted torches.

The Royal Mile is well named.   It is royal in origin and in history, and its exact length from the Castle drawbridge to the gate of Holyrood Palace is 1 mile 70 feet!

HOLYROODHOUSE

What Holyrood looked like when David I founded the Abbey there would be hard to picture with certainty, but he must have had an eye for its surrounding beauties as well as for its seclusion. To-day, the view from inside the Palace grounds is magnificent and presents an ingeniously contrived and pleasant illusion. The grassy banks are carried to the tops of the garden walls on the inside in such a way that the break between the enclosure and the surrounding " King's Park " —officially Holyrood Park—is not easily detected, and into the romantic grandeur of Arthur's Seat and Salisbury Crags the private grounds gently merge with spacious effect. It is hard to realize, against such a background, that one is within a few yards of drab industrialism and close-packed city life.

Even to walk from the Canongate through the ornamental iron gate into the grand forecourt is to arrive in another world, to step suddenly from the workaday into the legendary and the unreal. From the base of the statue of King Edward VII, the Peacemaker, the aspect is of Restoration French elegance, and the taste of the Merry Monarch, Charles II, is much in evidence inside and outside the Palace. The original Holyrood, the Abbey which now stands a roofless but picturesque ruin, was restored again and again after frequent depredations, and it is a museum piece of successive styles, touched up by Abbot Crawford in the fifteenth century, and later by Charles I and James VI. Its roof was in ruins in the eighteenth century, and an attempt to repair it met with disaster in a storm in 1768 which brought down the entire covering and left the skeleton which is now a familiar and much-loved part of the Edinburgh landscape. Inside this church, royal weddings took place, and there Charles I was crowned King of Scots. Headstones and slabs mark the graves of Scottish nobles, bishops and burghers. In the Royal Vault, whose repair was ordered by Queen Victoria, formerly lay embalmed the bodies of Scottish kings and queens, but in the Revolution of 1688 fanatics raided the tomb and scattered the royal bones.

Sometimes the Scottish Parliament met in the Abbey, sometimes on great royal occasions it became the scene of even more secular events, joustings and revels. One king, James II of Scotland, was born, married and buried within the Abbey walls. Royalty had early taken possession of its saintly ancestor's gift to the monks, and James IV had begun to establish a Palace there, work on which was continued for James V, whose daughter, Mary Queen of Scots, was to find here what turned out to be a tragic home. In her young days, the Palace was twice burnt by the English; and in Cromwell's days of occupation, it was burnt again. The Restoration brought it a new lease of life. Robert Mylne, King's Mason, built the entrance gateway in 1671 from designs by Sir William Bruce of Kinross, and Charles II took a personal interest in the interior decorations.

To-day the Palace is the occasional residence of the Royal Family. The King's Lord High Commissioner to the General Assembly of the Church of Scotland occupies the State Apartments each year when he visits the " Kirk's Parliament ", and royal investitures are sometimes held in the Palace. In the Portrait Gallery, on the inauguration of a new Parliament at Westminster, the Scottish Peers elect their representatives to sit in the House of Lords. The hereditary Keeper of the Palace is the Duke of Hamilton, who selects a Bailiff of Holyroodhouse. There is a body of Holyrood High Constables, in tasteful blue uniform with cockaded top hats, who share the regulation of the crowds on royal occasions with the King's Bodyguard, the Royal Society of Archers, while the State management of the premises is in the hands of the Office of Works.

Prince Albert, Consort of Queen Victoria, gave the forecourt (the old West Court) its beautiful centre-piece, the carved Gothic fountain. Passing beyond the majestic towered façade through the grand Carolean gateway, we come to the colonaded Inner Court, a quadrangle flanked by the Royal Apartments of modern usage on the right and the apartments associated with Mary Queen of Scots on the left. It is these latter, historical rooms which draw the sightseer, for here are the scenes of the murder of Rizzio—the bed in which the hapless Queen spent many a fearsome night, the private staircase trodden by her Scottish husbands, Darnley and Bothwell, and the nooks and crannies which hid conspirators and assassins. In the audience chamber the Martyr King, Charles I, slept, as did his venturesome descendant, Bonnie Prince Charlie, and his enemy, the Duke of Cumberland, who ended " Charlie's Year " with the defeat of the clans at Culloden. The chief curiosity of the Picture Gallery, dating from the Restoration period, is the collection of " portraits of Kings of Scotland " painted by the Flemish artist De Witt, who found his models in the streets of Edinburgh and adapted their passably Celtic profiles to represent imaginary monarchs stretching back as far as " Fergus I—330 B.C.". But the Palace has a number of Royal portraits of greater authenticity and merit.

" Queen Mary's Sun-dial ", in the gardens to the west of the chapel, has a dial on each of the twenty faces of its apex, but it is unlikely to have been there in Queen Mary's time and probably belongs to the reign of Charles I. " Queen Mary's Bath " is the name given to a lodge-like building at the north-west entrance of the Palace Yard. Here the Queen of Scots, according to local legend, used to bathe in milk or in white wine!

THE NEW TOWN

In the earlier years of the eighteenth century the Royal Mile and its back lanes comprised the town. A strip of ground lay between it and the wide and half-drained Burgh Loch to the south, while on the north side lay the Dolorous Valley of the Nor' Loch with its foreground of refuse heaps and slaughterhouses. We have to lift our hats to the pioneer town-planners, gentlemen representative of the Town Council and the professions, who met in 1752 to promote a scheme of expansion and new buildings. Their efforts led to the Act of Parliament of 1753, which gave powers to appoint Commissioners and made provision for the construction of important streets. The first fruits of the movement were the Royal Exchange buildings in the High Street.

Then came the North Bridge, the first great stride towards the realization of their dream of a new Edinburgh. It was begun in 1763 and its three 73-foot spans were completed in 1772. It was widened in 1876 and a new bridge built in its place in 1896-7.

While the erection of the first North Bridge went on, a quest was made for a complete plan for the New Town. In 1766 the project was thrown open to competition, and James Craig's design was accepted in the following year, when the Act to extend the royalty of the burgh was passed. In that year also—1767—the building of the New Town began, on the ridge, now crested by George Street, which runs parallel to the ridge of the Old Town, and is bounded on the east by another " horseshoe valley " to the west of Calton Hill.

The planners did not get things all their own way, and the plan as carried out was not quite so simple and symmetrical as Craig intended. Property rights stood in the way. St. Andrew Square, which was meant to face the New Town end of the North Bridge, had to move west, and the Earl of Moray's property and the boundary along the Queensferry Road blocked the West End. In the plan for George Street, St. George's Church, which faces east along the thoroughfare from the far side of Charlotte Square, was meant to be matched at the other end by St. Andrew's Church; but Sir Lawrence Dundas, the city's M.P., had secured that site for his mansion—his grand abode looking west into St. Andrew Square is now the home of the Royal Bank of Scotland and a very pleasing building, but it ousted St. Andrew's Church to a less picturesque position on the north side of George Street near the square. The planners were unsuccessful also in the long run in limiting the height of the buildings as the 1767 Act of the Council was designed to ensure. Despite the well-known fate of the best-laid schemes, however, George Street as it stands is a beautiful thoroughfare which does credit to the city.

In the New Town some of the best examples of the architectural work of Robert Adam, the local designer who rose most brilliantly to the opportunities presented by the plan, are to be found. The graceful façade of the Register House, an Adam building begun in 1774 to face the North Bridge, is thrown into the shade by the more gigantic General Post Office and the ornate vastness of the North British Hotel, but from the Post Office steps, or the pavement in front of the hotel, it is a gratifying sight with its grand staircase, its well-balanced lines and its tasteful and restrained ornamentation.

Adam's greatest memorial is the north side of Charlotte Square, which most strikingly preserves his studied lines and perfect use of stone. Built around 1790, its classical dignity and attractive cream colouring suggest the perfect square this might have been, but the place was completed some ten years after with another architect at work on the south side, and Adam's designs for the church were discarded. Nevertheless, Charlotte Square charms with its spaciousness and its quiet mood. The birthplace of Lord Haig, the World War I general, is marked by a tablet on the south side, and around the corner in Charlotte Street is the birthplace of Robert Bell, inventor of the telephone.

If your taste runs to monuments, George Street has an imposing row of them, from the equestrian tribute to Prince Albert, Queen Victoria's beloved Consort, nestling among the trees of Charlotte Square Garden, to that of Henry Dundas, Lord Melville, which faces it away at the other end, on its 136-feet-high pillar in the centre of

St. Andrew Square. At the junction of George Street and Castle Street, near Sir Walter Scott's house (39 Castle Street), Dr. Chalmers, one of Scotland's great theologians, stands in his robes with his Bible open before him. At the Frederick Street crossing the figure is of William Pitt; and at Hanover Street is the easily recognizable shape of King George IV, first of the Hanoverian line to pay a successful visit to the city, and inspirer of one of Edinburgh's most memorable outbursts of pageantry (with Sir Walter Scott prominent among its promoters).

Charlotte Square, George Street and St. Andrew Square accommodate many handsome office headquarters. The banks are well represented, as are the insurance companies and building societies, the Church of Scotland central organization, the National Bible Society (in St. Andrew Square), and some fine stores. The Masonic Hall between Castle Street and Frederick Street is a useful centre for lectures and concerts, and the Music Hall and Assembly Rooms, between Frederick Street and Hanover Street, are a favourite resort for ballroom and country dancing and for concerts.

The intersecting streets running up from Princes Street, crossing the ridge, and descending to Queen Street and the valley of the Water of Leith, are typically " Edinburgh " with their tenements, garrets and basement areas. Queen Street, in the earlier days of the New Town, was " the favourite Mall ", where strollers enjoyed the aspect of the wooded estates to the north, and the Firth of Forth and the hills of Fife beyond. Near St. David Street, its old Queen's Hall, easily identified by its prominent porch, has in its time been a lecture hall, a boxing stadium and a night club, but in 1930 became Broadcasting House, containing, besides studios, the administrative offices of the B.B.C.'s Scottish Regional Director.

Along from it to the east is the long ornamented building of the Scottish National Portrait Gallery and Museum of Antiquities, with many statues of famous Scots in niches on its outer walls, and a vast treasury of authentic portraits and relics of Scotland's past in orderly and educative array inside—one of a number of museums in the city which well repay a visit. It was a gift to the city by Mr. J. R. Findlay, a proprietor of *The Scotsman*.

Thistle Street, Hill Street and Young Street, running parallel to

George Street and Queen Street half-way between them, mingle business premises with dwellings in the Edinburgh style. Rose Street, the parallel thoroughfare nearer Princes Street, is celebrated most of all for its many public houses, and has a strong claim to being considered Edinburgh's " Bohemia ", where writers, painters, musicians, broadcasters and critics tend to forgather for the discussion of the arts, side by side with serious students of the bottle to whom such highbrow discourse perhaps has little appeal.

North, west and east from the central nucleus, the New Town continued to spread in the nineteenth century. North of Queen Street's gardens are Abercrombie Place, Heriot Row and Great King Street (in its lay-out something of a minor George Street), all part of the plan of Reid and Sibbald of 1804–6, built by about 1820. Moray Place and Ainslie Place followed as elegant West End efforts on awkward sites by Gillespie Graham. In 1822, recalls Henry Cockburn, the Earl of Moray's estate north of Charlotte Square began to be broken up for the building of these places, and " an open field with as green turf as Scotland could boast, with a few respectable trees on the flat, and thickly wooded on the bank along the Water of Leith ", gave way to rows of houses " where corncrakes used to rail ". It has been said that Gillespie Graham missed the opportunity presented by the Dean Valley when he made his houses face inwards. The West End further blossomed out in Maitland Street, Melville Street and crescents to the west, and the chief architectural feature of this area is the Episcopal Cathedral of St. Mary's, on generous Gothic lines.

Edinburgh from Calton Hill

PRINCES STREET

Whether or no Princes Street is the finest street in the world, as we natives love to hear the enthusiastic visitor rapturously proclaim, it certainly has its points. Purists make a fuss about its architectural inconsistencies. It has wandered somewhat from its original conception and is as much a museum of oddities, in its own way, as the Royal Mile. Staid Scottish buildings in rough stone stand side by side with extravagantly ornamented Victorian Gothic giants, like country cousins in hodden grey alongside excessively bejewelled *nouveaux riches*. Classical pillars and architraves vie with latter-day baronial, and both draw in their skirts, crowded by clashing chromium and shining black marble. But the discords do little to take away from Princes Street its overall beauty.

The Castle dominates the scene, lofty and aloof, and it is from this street that the most striking view of the vast, dark, rugged Rock and its irregular crown of antique buildings is to be obtained. The irregularity of the silhouette of Castle and Old Town make it almost impossible for architectural irregularity on the opposite side to spoil the scene, though the question is one for endless debate over cups of tea in one of these Princes Street cafés whose windows look out on to the enchanting scene beyond the valley.

Princes Street's shopping side has its own vitality and its own absorbing variety of interest. It is natural that such a site should have been besieged by commercial concerns with an eye to good business, and there is little in the way of shopping opportunity that is not to be found somewhere in its mile of mixed merchandise—though Lothian Road, The Bridges and Leith Street, and other thoroughfares, are also resplendent in attractive stores.

In almost rural contrast stands the south side of Princes Street, with never a shop along its length. Back from the street stands Princes Street Station with its broad-fronted, imposing Caledonian Hotel, known affectionately as " the Caley ", and on the corner of the south side of the main street, separated from the station hotel by Lothian Road, is the Episcopal Church of St. John's. Below and behind St. John's is one of Edinburgh's oldest kirks, St. Cuthbert's, whose original edifice arose under the shadow of the Rock in the very early days of the Castle's development. The modern St. Cuthbert's is conspicuous for the beauty of its interior equipment and decorations, which include an impressive carved frieze of the Last Supper behind the altar, after the famous Da Vinci painting.

It is surprisingly easy to turn from the hustle and bustle of Princes Street to the contemplative calm of this side with its churchyards and monuments and the pleasant gardens, and it is almost impossible to picture what the valley below the Rock on this side was like before the gardens were laid out. Cockburn recalls that " the great—indeed the vital improvement of enclosing, draining and ornamenting the valley to the west of the Mound (a part of the North Loch), for which a statute had been obtained in 1816, was completed in the autumn of 1820. Its value, or rather its glaring and indispensable necessity, can only be understood by those who knew, and who remember, what had become the dreadful, and apparently hopeless, condition of the ground. The place had just been sufficiently drained to prevent its ever again being a loch. But it was a nearly impassable, fetid marsh, a stinking swamp, open on all sides, the receptacle of many sewers, and seemingly of all the worried cats, drowned dogs and blackguardism of the city. Its abomination made it so solitary that the Volunteers used to practise ball-firing across it. The men stood on its north side and the targets were set up along the lower edge of the Castle hill or rock. The only difficulty was in getting across the swamp to place and examine the targets, which could be done only in very dry weather and at one or two places."

Nowadays this former swamp, the first piece of ground to be ornamented within the city outside of house-planted squares, is a sheltered and restful pleasure-ground which the citizens proudly share with the visitors. The steeply descending banks, beautifully laid out by the Parks Department under the direction of the City Gardener, shut off much of the noise of the street from the strollers on the broad level terrace and on the gravel paths, the sitters on the park benches and the lollers on the grassy slopes. For sunny days, of which Edinburgh gets a good share, there are pleasant leafy shades around the fountain with its coiling water nymphs and spouting heads, and its basin whose cool waters have an eternal allure for the young. The bandstand, centre-piece of the lower part of the garden, is used not only for band concerts but for the accompaniment of open-air dancing and the provision of varied stage entertainment. There are extensive and comfortable seating arrangements, as well as facilities for free listening and looking-on. Passers-by in the street above often crowd to the railing to share in sound and spectacle.

On the other side of the railway lines, crossed by bridges at convenient points, one can stroll amid the ruins of the Wellhouse Tower at the base of the Castle Rock, built in 1450 and a former source of water for the garrison, or enjoy the amenities of the green sward sloping down from the Castle Esplanade.

To return to the paved terrace, enjoyed for its sunny walk and its restful seats, the central attraction here is the Scottish-American War Memorial erected in 1927 by American Scots, and by United States admirers of Scotland and the Scots, in memory of those who fell in the First World War, and the national effort which supported them in their great fight. It consists of a striking bronze figure of a young Scot in uniform, seated looking towards the Castle, with a bronze frieze beyond representing the variety of Scots who went into battle, in a strong and well-designed setting of Craigleith stone. The originator of the idea was Mr. John Gordon Gray, a native of Scotland and a graduate of Aberdeen University, who was president of the St. Andrew's Society of Philadelphia. His appeal produced £10,000, though he died before the realization of his scheme. His successor as president, Mr. J. P. MacBean, carried on the project along with Dr. Ellis P. Oberholzer of the English-Speaking Union and Mr. John Gribbel, and the work was placed in the hands of a Philadelphia sculptor, Dr. R. Tait Mackenzie, who had designed memorials in the United States and in Canada. Sergeant-majors of the Highland Regiments advised the sculptor in the dressing of the figure, the frieze and statue were cast at the Roman Bronze Works in Brooklyn, and the stone was obtained at Ravelston in the north-west of the city. The American Ambassador of the day, the Hon. Alanson Bigelow Houghton, performed the dedication in 1927. A feature of the monument much appreciated by visitors is the thoughtful incorporation of stone seats in the design.

There are shelters farther along the terrace which are popular with the foot-weary sightseer. Near them the grand staircase takes the visitor past the Floral Clock, an annual display of floral arrangements with moving hands keeping the correct time and operated by chain from works accessible to the mechanics in the base of Allan Ramsay's statue. The Floral Clock is very naturally one of the favourite subjects of postcard views from Edinburgh.

The grand staircase leads us out to the Mound, the thoroughfare which winds up over the railway and round the foot of Castle Hill into the Old Town. It was formerly " the Earthern Mound ", and was started in 1783, as a second link between the Old and New Towns, to match the North Bridge, and as a convenient dumping ground for the earth excavated from the basements of the New Town houses. In 1780 it was calculated that 1,300,000 cartloads of earth had already been dumped here.

Now the Mound displays two of the city's handsome Grecian buildings, from designs of W. H. Playfair, the Royal Scottish Academy (built 1823–36), facing Princes Street, and the Scottish National Gallery (1850–8) just behind it, both of them art galleries used for the presentation of pictures old and new. The collection in the National Gallery is a most informative introduction to the history of art in Scotland against its international background, and the Diploma Collection at the rear of the Academy is also of value for an understanding of art appreciation, while the annual shows of new paintings in the Academy, for which it was designed, and the frequent special exhibitions of British and foreign art for which both buildings are utilized, make the Mound the magnet of the artistically minded.

The square on the east side of the Mound is the " Hyde Park " of Edinburgh, where orators for a hundred causes draw their eagerly listening and often vocally critical audiences—an interesting place for the curious stroller to sidle into on a Sunday night. If you have a taste for debate, sane or fantastic, and are prepared to hear something which may provoke you to interjection and involve you in a heated argument, the Mound is your place.

East Princes Street Garden is noted for its floral displays, and it has a grand terrace and pleasant by-paths and bowling greens. It contains the Scott Monument, in which the white Carrara marble figure of Sir Walter, with his staghound Maida at his feet, sits looking up St. David Street, surmounted by a grandiose Gothic spire on four arches, ascended by a narrow interior stair, leading to a museum and a series of balconies which give excellent views of the city and farther afield. There are 287 steps, and you can obtain a certificate to testify that you have climbed them. Characters from Scott's Waverley Novels are represented by the statues in niches on the outside walls of this 200-feet-high elaboration, designed by George M. Kemp and erected in 1840–4 at a cost of £15,650, raised by public subscription.

David Livingstone's monument on the terrace farther east is much visited by overseas admirers of the Scottish medical missionary, who died in Africa after a great career of service to humanity.

Another crossing into the Old Town, the Waverley Bridge, bounds this garden on the east, leading to Cockburn Street by the back of the City Chambers, and to Market Street, which winds under the southern-most span of the North Bridge. Crossing the wide opening of the Waverley Bridge on our Princes Street stroll we come to the Waverley Market, whose roof at Princes Street level is railed off from us. This building, which occupies part of the steep slope down into the railway valley, is bounded on its eastern side by the famous Waverley Steps, down which people of all the nations have sped to their trains—it is a notorious spot for powerful winds, and there are times when the assistance of the police is required to rescue foot-passengers from the compelling blast.

The Waverley Station grew up in the early part of the nineteenth century, displacing markets, Trinity Church and Hospital, and the old Physic Garden in which eighteenth-century beaux used to strut. Part of it occupies the eastern end of what was once the Nor' Loch. The Edinburgh & Glasgow Railway and the North British Railway held the western and eastern sides respectively, but amalgamated in 1865, and in the following year the amalgamated railway company undertook to

4

construct a new fruit and vegetable market on ground adjoining Princes Street and the Waverley Bridge. The Waverley Market was completed and handed over to the City Corporation in 1869, paved with granite setts, but without roof or covering. After 1874 the Corporation, at a cost of £30,834, improved the market, roofed it over and made internal arrangements for stands, stalls and shops, with the ground floor as a market-place and premises opening off the surrounding gallery. The Waverley Market is frequently used for shows, menageries and the like, and the annual circus and carnival at Christmas and New Year is an inseparable part of the city life, but it is one of the conditions of letting that due provision has to be made for the requirements of the market gardeners. As a consequence of this association, Market Street north of the station continued to be the " Covent Garden " of Edinburgh, and a number of fruit and flower warehouses grew up there.

Like the " Caley " at the other end of the street, the North British Hotel is much in demand for big dinners, of which Edinburgh has a number of traditional ones. The General Post Office, beyond the North Bridge opening, arose in 1858 on the site of a former Theatre Royal.

Waterloo Place, with its bridge over the Calton valley, opened up the way to the east, and to the sea at Portobello, after the 1814 Act. It made the access to Calton Hill easier and also opened a way to Calton Jail, the building of which was begun some years earlier to replace the High Street jail known as " The Heart of Midlothian ". Some critics of the time thought it was the height of bad taste to give so glorious an eminence as the Calton crags, which now overlook the railway lines, to a prison. Cockburn said, " It was one of our noblest sites, and would have been given by Pericles to one of his finest edifices ". The old Calton Jail used to look like a second Castle on that craggy cliff, but its iron-barred windows and its associations were not pleasant. However, between World Wars I and II, the jail came down to make way for a fine edifice which would probably have gladdened the heart of Lord Cockburn—St. Andrews' House, home of the Scottish Office and seat of Government north of the Tweed. Here, in a room panelled with walnut said to be from a tree planted by Mary Queen of Scots, sits the Secretary of State for Scotland when he officiates in the city, and here the various Scottish Government Departments have their headquarters. The Governor's House of the old jail survived the general demolition, and its castellated style is picturesque as seen from North Bridge. In the Calton burial ground stand a monument to Abraham Lincoln, erected in 1893, and an obelisk erected in 1844 to political martyrs. There is a rather inadequate monument to Robert Burns on the terrace farther east overlooking the north back of the Canongate, but the Royal High School, built in Doric style in 1825 at a cost of £30,000, makes full use of the opportunities offered by the terraced hill slope. On the crest of Calton Hill are the old City Observatory, the Dugald Stewart Monument, and that remarkable group of pillars, the National Monument, locally nicknamed " Edinburgh's Disgrace ". From the point of view of scenic beauty it is no disgrace. Along with the telescope-like tower, 102 feet high, in memory of Lord Nelson, it is a characteristic part of the " Edinburgh sky-line ", although, like many a so-called " Folly " in other parts of the world, it is unfinished. It was first projected in 1816 to commemorate the triumphs of the Napoleonic War, but the original plan was simply for a pillar, then the scheme expanded to envisage a complete " Temple of Minerva ". The subscription list rose to £17,000, but £60,000 was the estimate for the whole project. It is a brave relic of the days when Edinburgh loved her title, " The Modern Athens ", and Calton Hill has the most Athenian air of all the city areas.

THE SOUTH SIDE

Princes Street and the Royal Mile naturally take up much of the visitor's time, but it is a rewarding adventure to follow the line of The Bridges, the Lothian Road or George IV Bridge out south. The Bridges attract as a fine modern shopping centre, but they also lead us to the part of the University known as the Old Quadrangle, another satisfying relic of the work of Robert Adam. Edinburgh University is a far-flung institution, and this part houses mainly the Arts and Law Faculties, and the very fine libraries, as well as the central offices. It is the successor to the Town's College founded in 1582 on the site of Kirk of Field, where Darnley was murdered. Following on the opening of South Bridge in 1785, the foundation stone of the present University building was laid in 1789. Adam's design was somewhat modified in execution and it took fifty years to complete the work. Both the High School and the Infirmary were quite near here at one time, but both are now far sundered from their original sites.

Adjacent Chambers Street commemorates its founder, William Chambers, Lord Provost in 1865, celebrated for his work on the City Improvement Act of 1867. It includes Minto House, a part of the University, the substantial and well-equipped Heriot-Watt College for technical students, and the Royal Scottish Museum, a vast building distinguished for its collections of machinery, animal habitats, potteries, sculptural specimens, models, and historical and geographical exhibits. It has also proved a plastic medium for the presentation of special exhibitions from time to time.

A short walking distance to the west from the Old Quad is the New Quad, the home of Edinburgh's famous Medical School (not forgetting the Royal College of Surgeons slightly to the south of the Old Quad). Adjoining the New Quad is the McEwan Hall, in which graduation ceremonies of all faculties take place and academic gatherings are held, and from whose distinguished platform many famous men—

from Thomas Carlyle, philosopher and writer, to Alistair Sim, actor and comedian—have addressed the students as their elected Lord Rectors.

Also in this vicinity is the University Union, the social centre of the male students of all faculties, with its fine debating hall, libraries, recreation rooms, and dining-rooms. Behind it is lovely George Square, started in 1766 as the speculation of a builder named Brown and at one time subsequently a centre of Edinburgh society. It contains the College of Agriculture, Cowan House residence for students, the University Women's Union and a tastefully laid-out garden.

West from the New Quad in Lauriston Place, is the Royal Infirmary of Edinburgh, a vast effort in the Scotch Baronial style which is so characteristic of our city, with Functionalist additions in the more modern wings. Opposite the Infirmary is George Heriot's School, in its extensive grounds, built between 1628 and 1650 from the bequest of the famous jeweller to King James VI and Queen Anne. Heriot died in 1624 and left the residue of his estate to the Town Council to build and endow a hospital for the maintenance and education of poor children. The sum, amounting to £23,625 10s. 3½d., was collected by the Town Council and administered by them, shrewdly invested and considerably increased. George Heriot's noble example has been followed by other merchants since, and by groups of merchants and traders, with the result that the city is rich in endowed schools providing first-class education.

Behind the new University buildings and the Infirmary stretches the public park known as the Meadows, with its famous Middle Meadow Walk and its Jaw-bone Walk, so named after the whale's jaw-bone which arches one end and is a relic of an exhibition. The Meadows occupy the site of the old Burgh Loch or South Loch, which was a natural sheet of water. Thomas Hope in 1722 drained and planted the district known as Hope Park on the eastern side. Bruntsfield Links at the western end, and on the other side of the fine green-flanked thoroughfare of Melville Drive, were cleared of whins and old quarries by the unemployed in 1816, at the same time as the walks were laid out on Calton Hill and a path was cleared along the base of Salisbury Crags —an early example of public works to relieve poverty.

The Meadows have played a great part in the past in developing cricket in the city, and the Links likewise have contributed to the development of golf.

The most convenient way to the Infirmary and its hinterland from the city is by the Mound and George IV Bridge. This bridge was raised in 1827 and has ten arches, almost all of them hidden by buildings. Its thoroughfare gives convenient access to the Grassmarket, one-time cattle market of the city, and to the West Port, scene of the notorious Burke and Hare murders, which came to light in 1828 after these two rascals, in the course of a year or two, had murdered about sixteen people in order to sell their bodies to anatomists, a fact which Burke confessed after his conviction on one murder charge. Hare turned King's evidence against his associate. The case cast a grave shadow on the reputation of one of Edinburgh's leading anatomists, Dr. Knox, who, according to Sir Robert Christison, " had rather wilfully shut his eyes to incidents which ought to have excited the grave suspicions of a man of his intelligence ", and whom Sir Walter Scott categorized as " one who has had so lately the boldness of trading in human flesh ". Yet in his day Knox was the most popular lecturer on anatomy in the city.

Just off George IV Bridge at the top of Candlemaker Row is Greyfriars Churchyard, and near it, over a drinking-fountain, is a statue to " Greyfriars Bobby ", the dog that refused to leave his master's grave.

George IV Bridge accommodates the Central Library, known as the " Carnegie ", the headquarters of a chain of civic libraries which make good books on all subjects readily accessible to readers without fee. It also gives access to the National Library of Scotland, formerly the Advocates' Library, a great repository of manuscripts and reference books of all kinds. The street has a number of famous old bookshops, as have Bristol Place and Teviot Place nearer the University. This is certainly a district of learning, and students and professors are conspicuous among its browsers. The College of Art is in Lady Lawson Street beyond the West Port, and is yet another valuable part of the city's great cultural equipment.

Lothian Road, another of the main thoroughfares leading south, has in Lothian House, on the site of the old canal port near Fountainbridge, a handsome building which, like St. Andrew's House, was built to accommodate Government Departments, but also houses some fine shops.   Tollcross, to the south, is yet another busy shopping centre. Off Lothian Road is the Usher Hall, the principal concert hall of the city.

The way along Lothian Road takes you eventually to Churchhill and Morningside, districts to which the lure of the sun drew the citizens of the expanding town in the nineteenth century. South of the Meadows also lie Marchmont, with its impressive " Baronial " tenements and its traditional attraction for the student boarder, and the splendid villa districts of Grange and Mortonhall. The Bridges route leads out to similar residential areas in Mayfield, Newington, Liberton and beyond, areas representing successive extensions of the city from the middle of the nineteenth century until 1920, when the original burgh of 138 acres had expanded to 32,402 acres!

LEITH

The leftward fork at the east end of Princes Street past the Register House is Leith Street, which curves eventually into Leith Walk, the steep, broad thoroughfare laid out in the late eighteenth century to improve communications between the New Town and the adjacent burgh and seaport of Leith.

Pilrig was until 1920 the city boundary, for although Edinburgh in its early charters had the superiority of the port and although the city was always heavily dependent on its maritime and commerical adjunct, Leith long fought against absorption, and, even after the New Town had brought the city closer to it in a geographical sense, in 1833 the seaport town succeeded in becoming a parliamentary burgh. The Greater Edinburgh Act of 1920, however, led to the dissolution of the Town Council of Leith and the joint trusts responsible for the port, and their functions were transferred to a new and enlarged Edinburgh Town Council. It was an expensive Act, costing £51,771 to promote, and the compensation to dispossessed officials amounted to a further £50,337, but the amalgamation was logical and in the long run an economy. Nevertheless, " Leithers " are still regarded, and regard themselves, as a people apart, and the taking over of the seaport town by its big neighbour has not succeeded in obliterating the character of the adopted burgh.

Naturally Leith has played a big part in the history of Edinburgh. The wealth of the city came in large part from the port, and to-day much of the industrial strength of Edinburgh is derived from Leith.

Even in the unsettled years of the Wars of Independence, the Scottish patriot Sir William Wallace was able to assure the merchants of Europe that they could trade direct with Scotland through the port of Leith. In Reformation times, when the religious war among the Scots was welcomed by Queen Elizabeth as minimizing the possibility of her northern neighbour giving aid to her enemies on the Continent, that

Adams Houses, North Side of Charlotte Square

shrewd strategist sent English troops to assist the Protestant Scots to besiege the French garrison of the port. It was at Leith that Mary Queen of Scots put in when she arrived from France to take up her tragic reign, and from there she journeyed to Holyrood on horseback. And it was in Leith that Cromwell set up his Citadel to command Edinburgh, making the burghers up in the Royal Mile groan under the burden of its erection and upkeep.

Apart from its value as a port giving direct access to the ports of Europe, Leith early established its industrial importance, with its mills on the Water of Leith—" the Mills of Leith " of Edinburgh's 1329 Charter; and to-day the formerly independent burgh is the city's most industrialized district. It has extensive docks with modern facilities for unloading cargo vessels and adequate railway and other transport provisions at hand; and its business premises are not confined to the warehouses, cold stores, and coastal-shipping offices which one naturally expects to find at a port. Its huge granaries are striking landmarks seen from far up in Edinburgh, and its flour mills likewise are an integral part of the city landscape. Some of the biggest factories in the East of Scotland are to be found here, and whisky is made and blended as well as stored in the port. Oil-cake factories, a big seed concern, a rope-walk, engineering works, food manufactories, glass works, chemical factories—the list of industries represented, on an extensive scale, surprises with its wealth and variety.

Even from the sightseeing point of view, the docks are well worth a visit, and Leith Links preserve one of several green spots among all this sometimes drab industrialism. A picturesque aspect is the mouth of the Water of Leith with its big colony of swans.

GREEN PASTURES

If your hunger is for the wide open spaces, Edinburgh has plenty of them, all within easy reach of the centre of the town. Arthur's Seat itself, and its attendant Salisbury Crags, which dominate the view to the east of the city, are ideal for a stroll. If climbing—or hill-walking, not quite so strenuous—is your fancy, the extinct volcano invites with its green slopes and rocky cliffs; and if even a mild stroll over the shoulder of the minor mountain is too much of a task in decent holiday weather, there is the broad King's Park to saunter in at ease, with benches in good number on which to rest and take in the scene.

Arthur's Seat rises to over 822 feet, and its leonine silhouette has led the peak to be known also as the Lion's Head. Between the Head and the Lion's Haunch, or Nether Hill, which is still 750 feet above sea-level, is a favourite steep route down the Gutted Haddie past Ravens Craig. The Crow Hill and the Whinny Hill ("whinny" meaning gorse-clad) are lesser promontories to the north. West of Arthur's Seat stretches Hunter's Bog, with its rifle-range up to 600 yards giving a rough measure of the distance between Arthur's Seat and the Salisbury Crags, which attain a height of 500 feet. The walk along the foot of the Crags by means of the Radical Road is popular with Edinburgh folk, and when there are garden parties inside the Palace grounds at Holyroodhouse, the slopes at the northern base of the Crags give the best vantage point for a view of the gay scene.

Whether Arthur's Seat has any connexion with the sixth-century British hero-king is a moot point. The name "Arthurissete" goes back hundreds of years, yet some have sought to derive it from "Ard-nan-Sith", height of the fairy knolls, or "Ard-na-saighde", height of the arrow (because, presumably, of its advantages for the practice of archery). The district was Welsh (ancient British) before it was either Gaelic or Anglic, and there is no reason why it should not have

Hill, which local country folk used to call " Kirkyetton ". This wild and windy hill is associated with Robert Louis Stevenson, who lived at nearby Swanston Cottage, which his family had as their summer residence from 1867 (when he was 17) until 1880, and where W. E. Henley, whom Stevenson first met in Edinburgh Royal Infirmary, stayed when he and Robert Louis collaborated as playwrights.

Inverleith Park, another green spot, this time to the north of the city, also has associations with the great teller of tales. Beyond the adjoining Royal Botanic Gardens, which were transplanted here from their original site in Leith Walk in 1823, is Howard Place, where, at No. 8, R. L. S. was born on November 13, 1850, as the R.L.S. Club and Museum at the spot serve to recall.

Yet another much frequented walk is the Rest and Be Thankful Road over Corstorphine Hill round the back of the Scottish Zoological Park. Another is from Cramond across the ferry provided by the Earl of Rosebery and through his beautifully wooded Dalmeny to South Queensferry and the Forth Bridge. Cramond is in fact a grand starting point for many entrancing walks. The promenade along the sea-front is beautifully laid out, and gives a grand view of the islands in the Firth and the Fife coast. The nearby public park at Lauriston Castle is a further charming attraction.

Saughton Park, on the Water of Leith in the west of the city, has beautiful rose gardens. For a taste of country in the heart of the town, you should go below the Dean Bridge by the road through the quaint Old Dean Village, and travel along the wooded gorge by the river past St. Bernard's Well, an old resort for those who fancied " taking the waters ". Another grand walk, with rewarding architectural sights as well as natural scenic beauties, is round from Dean by John Watson's Institution and the Orphan Hospital, by Ravelston and Stewart's College to Queensferry Road, and down Orchard Brae to Comely Bank, where Fettes College completes the series of educational buildings testifying to the public spirit and taste of their founders.

THE OUTSKIRTS

Some of the most important parts of Edinburgh are out on the fringe of the city. For instance, the extensive area known as Gorgie, west of Haymarket Station, is highly industrialized, and its Corn Market, Slaughterhouses and Cattle Market extend over 25 acres beyond Hutchison Road, and have direct communication with two railways. These premises were completed and opened in 1910, the undertaking, including the railway connexions and sidings, costing £112,000. On the recreational side, Gorgie includes Tynecastle Park, noted as the home of one of the city's two leading football clubs, the Heart of Midlothian. The other leading club, Hibernian F.C., has its headquarters in Easter Road, north of London Road in the Calton district. Rivalry between these two clubs and their followers is friendly but intense, and their fortunes in the Scottish Cup and League competitions are a leading topic of conversation among the citizens throughout the winter months. Near Tynecastle, in Murrayfield, is the Scottish Rugby Union ground, where enthusiasts carrying plaids and travelling rugs flock to see big "international" clashes between Scotland and England, Ireland or Wales. Near Stenhouse, towards the big housing district of Sighthill, is Saughton Prison, a modern institution with, one is told, many amenities, built out in the green belt to replace Calton Jail, which made way for St. Andrew's House in Waterloo Place.

Corstorphine, another big residential area in the extreme west of the city, is mostly noted for the Scottish Zoological Park on one of its sunny and wooded slopes. The variety of animals who find the air of Corstorphine congenial after a period of acclimatization in a house set apart for that purpose, and the extent to which the natural surroundings have been adapted to provide spacious dens for lions, pools for bears and sea-lions, and ponds for the aquatic birds, make this the mecca of the sightseer from home and abroad. It has a first-class aquarium, containing fish from the rivers and coastal waters of Scotland as well as from foreign parts, and its clubhouse, restaurant and band-stand add to the comforts of the enthusiast for zoology.

Some of the city's hospitals make good use of the healthy surround-ings in the outlying parts, and a number of educational institutions also have found ideal settings on the fringe. George Watson's College, which has produced many outstanding scholars and public men, is to the south-west along the Colinton Road, and the Training College for Roman Catholic women teachers is at the Convent of the Sacred Heart on the quiet slopes of Craiglockhart.

In West Mains Road towards Liberton is yet another part of the far-flung University, King's Buildings, housing chemistry, geology, zoology and engineering departments, and the piggeries, sheep and goat houses, and other appurtenances of the animal-breeding research department. Here the Institute of Animal Genetics and the Imperial Bureau of Animal Genetics have done valuable work in a branch of science important to humanity at large. Around ruined Craigmillar Castle to the south of Arthur's Seat, and towards Melville Castle beyond Liberton, and also on the Portobello Road, are extensive nurseries representing yet another trade in which the city has a good foothold.

On the sea-front, in addition to Leith, Edinburgh has the well-equipped harbour of Granton, and the little fishing village of Newhaven, which still preserves its individuality although so closely linked with the city. Sir James Wilson, the leading authority on the dialects of Lowland Scotland, found in Newhaven a dialect quite distinct from that of Edinburgh or the Lothians, and while it is now a joke, among the Newhaven folk themselves, that they regard the Edinburghers and the Leithers as " foreigners ", it is not so long since it was a reality. New-haven has a busy fish market, and its Fisherwomen's Choir, in their attractive traditional costume, is one of the musical prides of the city. Granton's trawler fleet lands hundreds of thousands of hundredweights of white fish in a year, and its coal-loading plant plays a big part in the city's export trade—Edinburgh and district being more and more a coal-producing area, and Leith and Granton being its direct channels of communication with Europe, and with the English coast.

Portobello, as well as being a seaside holiday town, with a fine open-air bathing pool and amusements parks, is an industrial area, and its power station is a substantial contributor to the supply of electricity through the grid for both domestic and industrial purposes. This coastal suburb, by the way, was the birthplace of the late Sir Harry Lauder, the minstrel boy of Scotland, whose kilt and crooked stick waggled humorously around the world from Broadway to Sydney and farther afield on many a world tour of Scottish song and jesting.

The tale is told that Sir Harry once returned to his native town to give a performance, and the Portobello audience listened to his jokes in silence. Lauder, so the story goes, thought he had " flopped ", but the manager of the show cried enthusiastically, " Man, Harry, ye were immense! They loved ye! It was a' they could do to keep frae laughin' out loud!"

I know the story is not at all true; it is one of many variations on the theme of the Scot's slowness to respond to a joke. But it may help to comfort the visitor to Edinburgh who finds the traditional phlegm of the Scot—especially the east-coast Scot—sometimes upsetting. As the Lauder of the story would surely have known, the Edinburgh folk like you, and they are glad to be in your company, though they may not be very demonstrative about it.

464